PIANO / VOCAL / GUITAR

CANCIONES DE AMOR
(LATIN LOVE SONGS)

ISBN 0-7935-9306-9

HAL•LEONARD®
CORPORATION

7777 W. BLUEMOUND RD. P.O. BOX 13819 MILWAUKEE, WI 53213

Visit Hal Leonard Online at
www.halleonard.com

CONTENTS

ALWAYS IN MY HEART
(Siempre En Mi Corazón)

Music and Spanish Words by ERNESTO LECUONA
English Words by KIM GANNON

There's no moun-tain top so high that some-how love can't climb, no, no, true love will find a way.

There's no riv-er quite so wide that love can't cross in

AMOR
(Amor, Amor, Amor)

Music by GABRIEL RUIZ
Spanish Words by RICARDO LOPEZ MENDEZ
English Words by NORMAN NEWELL

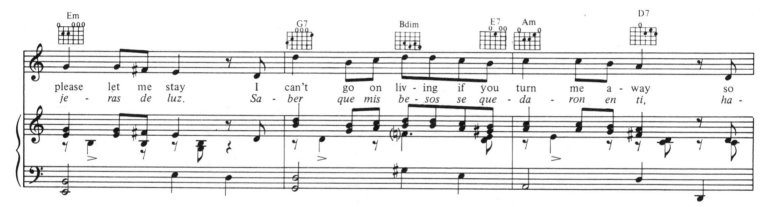

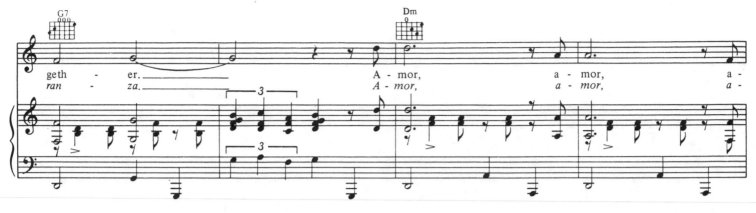

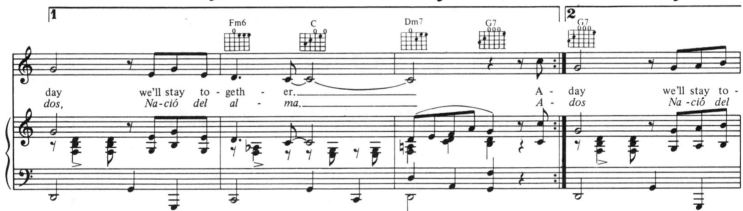

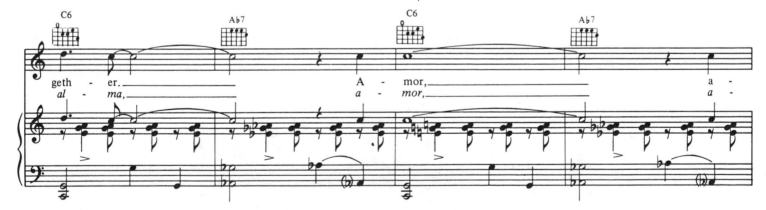

AQUELLOS OJOS VERDES
(Green Eyes)

Music by NILO MENENDEZ
Spanish Words by ADOLFO UTRERA
English Words by E. RIVERA and E. WOODS

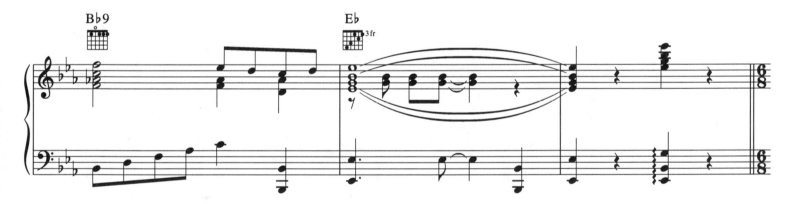

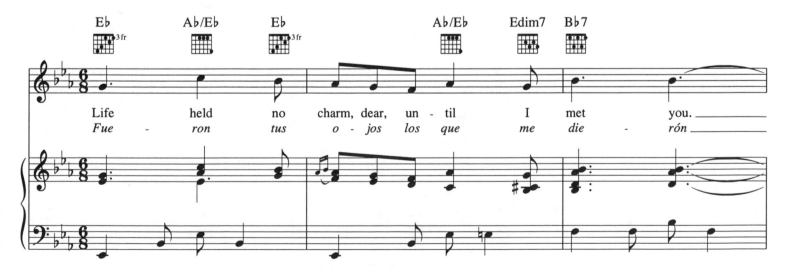

Life held no charm, dear, un - til I met you. _____
Fue - ron tus o - jos los que me die - rón _____

ANEMA E CORE
(With All My Heart)

English Lyric by MANN CURTIS and HARRY AKST
Italian Lyric by TITO MANLIO
Music by SALVE D'ESPOSITO

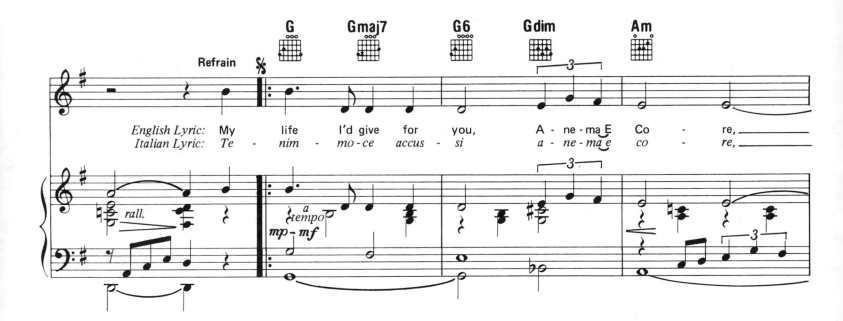

English Lyric: My life I'd give for you, A-ne-ma E Co-re,
Italian Lyric: Te nim-mo-ce accus-si a-ne-ma e co-re,

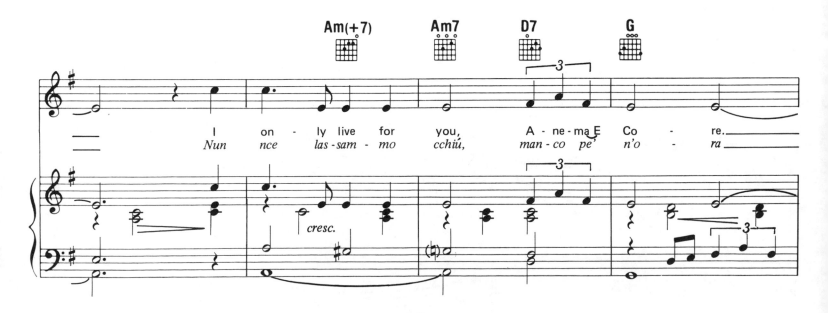

I on-ly live for you, A-ne-ma E Co-re.
Nun nce las-sam-mo cchiú, man-co pe' n'o-ra

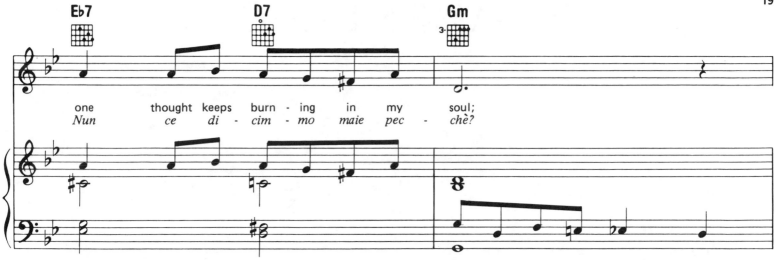

one thought keeps burn-ing in my soul;
Nun ce di - cim - mo maie pec - chè?

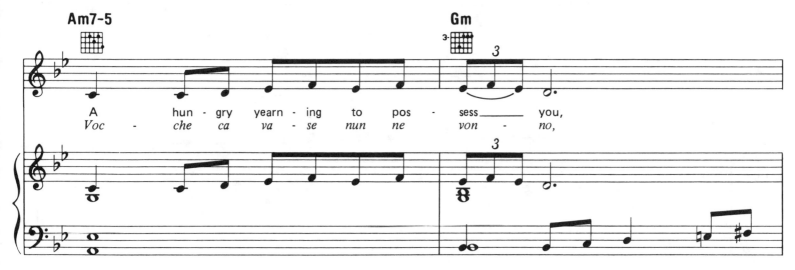

A hun-gry yearn-ing to pos-sess_____ you,
Voc - che ca va - se nun ne von - no,

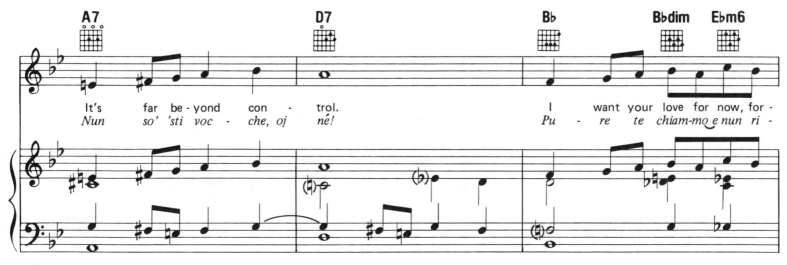

It's far be-yond con-trol. I want your love for now, for-
Nun so' 'sti voc - che, oj né! Pu - re te chiam-mo e nun ri -

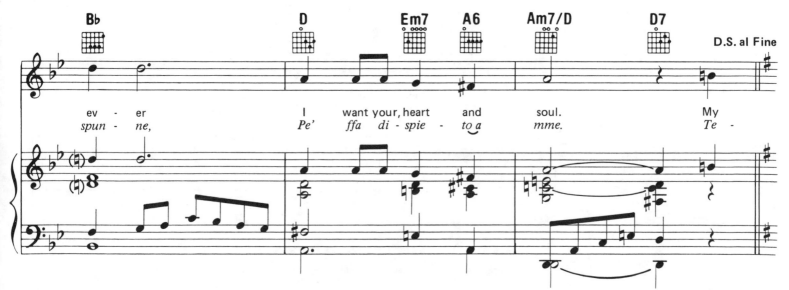

D.S. al Fine

ev - er I want your, heart and soul. My
spun - ne, Pe' ffa di - spie - to a mme. Te -

BÉSAME MUCHO
(Kiss Me Much)

Music and Spanish Words by
CONSUELO VELAZQUEZ
English Words by SUNNY SKYLAR

A DAY IN THE LIFE OF A FOOL
(Manha De Carnaval)

Words by CARL SIGMAN
Music by LUIZ BONFA

Slowly, with a Bossa Nova beat

A day _____ in the life _____ of a fool,
Ma - nhã _____ tão bo - ni - ta ma - nhã.

_____ a sad _____ and a long, _____ lone - ly
De um di - a fe - liz _____ que che -

day. _____
gou. _____

I walk the av - e - nue _____
O sol ne céu sur - giu _____

THE BREEZE AND I

Words by AL STILLMAN
Music by ERNESTO LECUONA

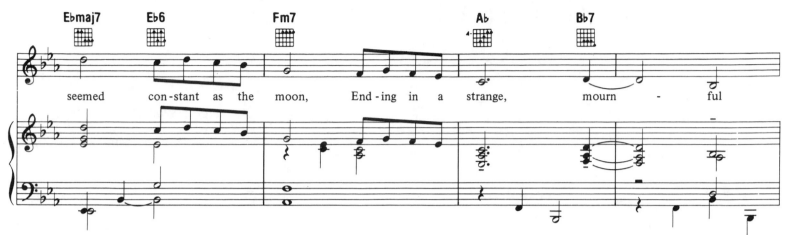

seemed con-stant as the moon, End-ing in a strange, mourn - ful

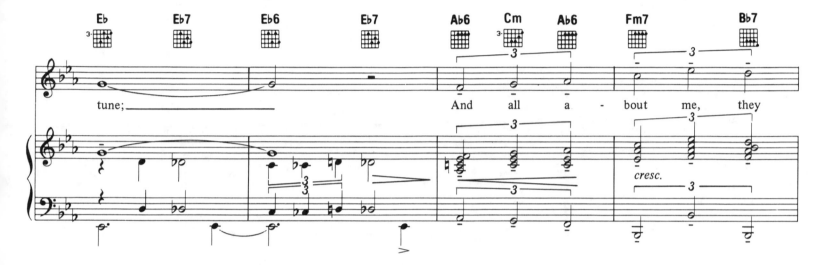

tune; _____ And all a - bout me, they

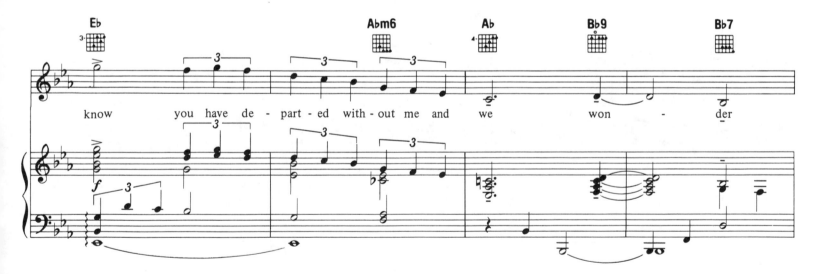

know you have de - part - ed with-out me and we won - der

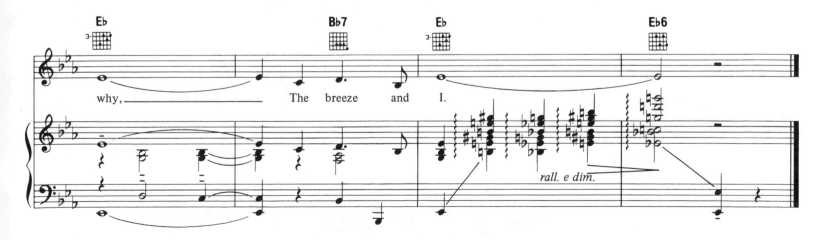

why, _____ The breeze and I.

CHERRY PINK AND APPLE BLOSSOM WHITE

French Words by JACQUES LARUE
English Words by MACK DAVID
Music by LOUIGUY

Rhumba

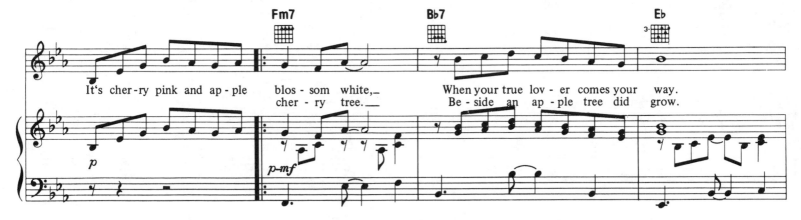

It's cher-ry pink and ap-ple blos-som white,__ When your true lov-er comes your way.
cher-ry tree.__ Be-side an ap-ple tree did grow.

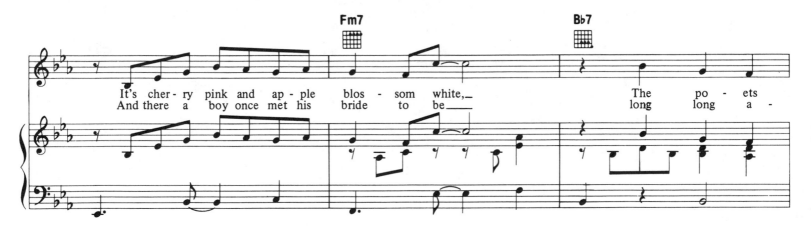

It's cher-ry pink and ap-ple blos-som white,__ The po-ets
And there a boy once met his bride to be___ long long a-

say. The sto-ry goes that once a go The boy looked

in - to her eyes, It was a sight to en-thrall, The breez-es joined in their sighs, The blos-soms start-ed to fall. And as they

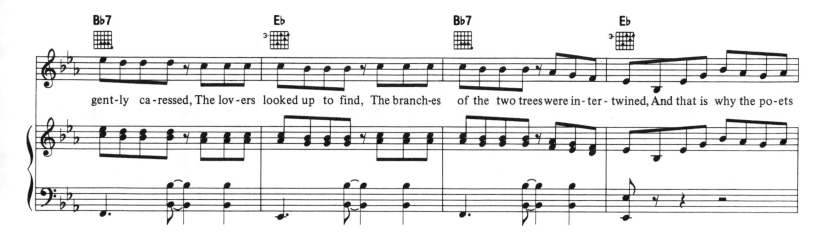

gent-ly ca-ressed, The lov-ers looked up to find, The branch-es of the two trees were in-ter-twined, And that is why the po-ets

al - ways write,_ If there's a new moon bright a - bove, It's cher-ry pink and ap - ple

blos - som white,_ When you're in love._

DAMISELA ENCANTADORA

Music and Spanish Lyric by
ERNESTO LECUONA

Moderate Waltz

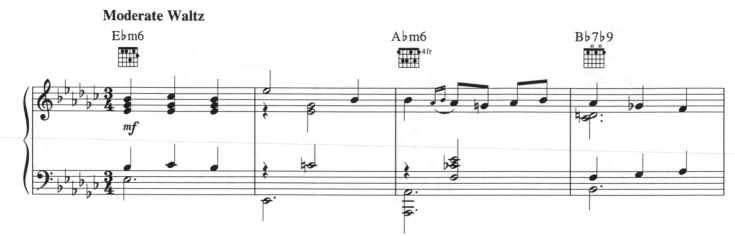

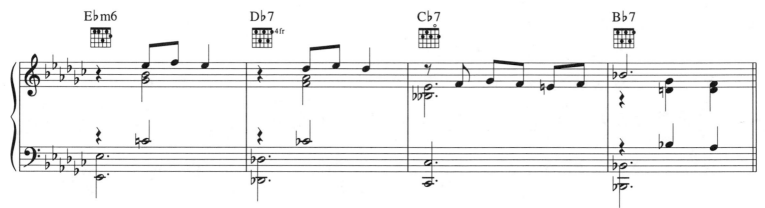

Por tus o - ja - zos ne - gros, __ lle - nos de a - mor, por tu bo -
Cuan - do a ti los ga - la - nes __ sin dis - tin - ción te de - di -

aui - ta ro - ja, __ que es u - na flor, por tu cuer - po de pal -
can re - quie - bros __ con gran pa - sión, con tu ai - re de prin -

me-ra, ___ lin-do y gen-til se mue-re mi co-ra-zón. _____
ce-sa, ___ be-llo y jun-cal, des tro-zas mi co-ra-zón. _____

___ Si me qui-sie - ras, fi-gu - li - na de A -
___ Si tu me die - ras tus ca - ri - cias de a -

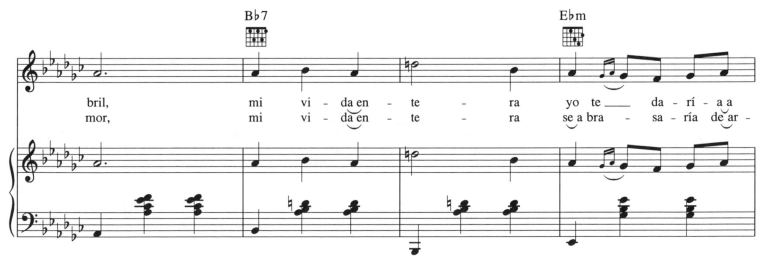

bril, mi vi-da en-te - ra yo te___ da-rí - a a
mor, mi vi-da en-te - ra se a bra - sa-ría de ar -

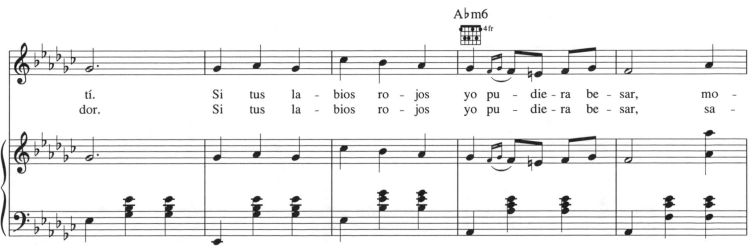

tí. Si tus la-bios ro-jos yo pu-die-ra be-sar, mo-
dor. Si tus la-bios ro-jos yo pu-die-ra be-sar, sa-

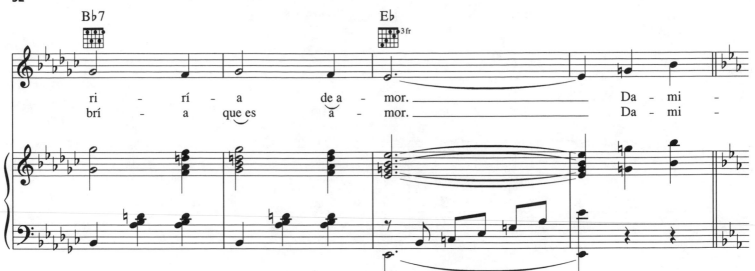

ri - rí - a de a - mor. _____ Da - mi -
brí - a que es a - mor. _____ Da - mi -

se - la en - can - ta - do - ra, _____ da - mi - se - la, por

tí yo mue - ro. _____ Si me mi - ras,

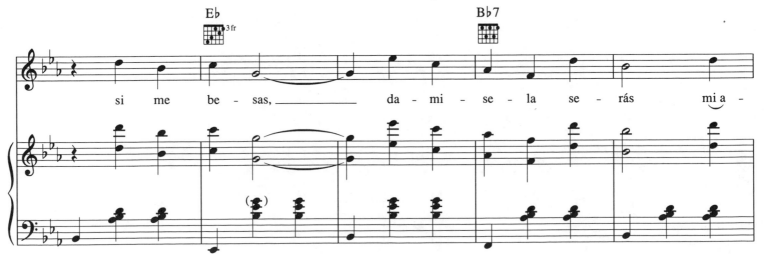

si me be - sas, _____ da - mi - se - la se - rás mi a -

mor. _____ Da - mi - se - la en - can - ta - do - ra, _____

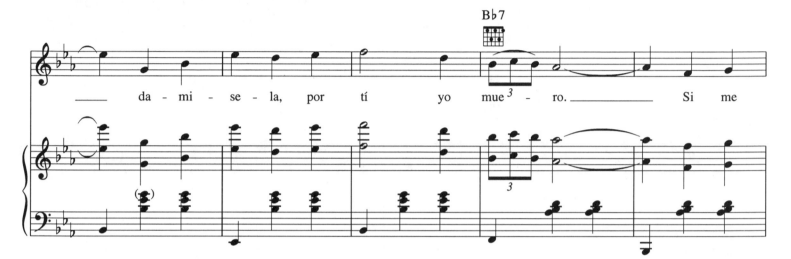

___ da - mi - se - la, por tí yo mue - ro. _____ Si me

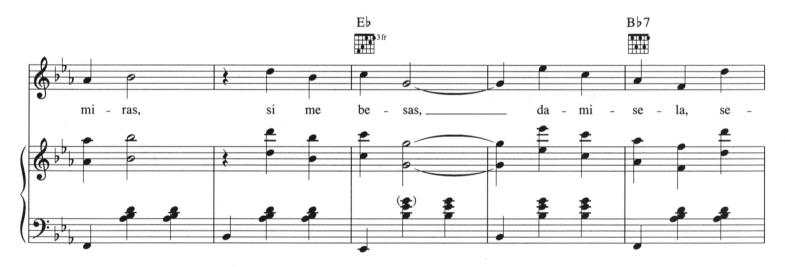

mi - ras, si me be - sas, _____ da - mi - se - la, se -

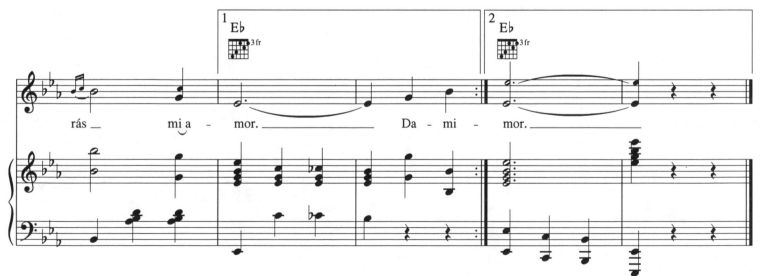

rás ___ mi a - mor. _____ Da - mi - mor.

EL RELICARIO
(Shrine of Love)

English Words by CAROL RAVEN
Spanish Words by OLIVEROS Y CASTELIVI
Music by JOSE PADILLA

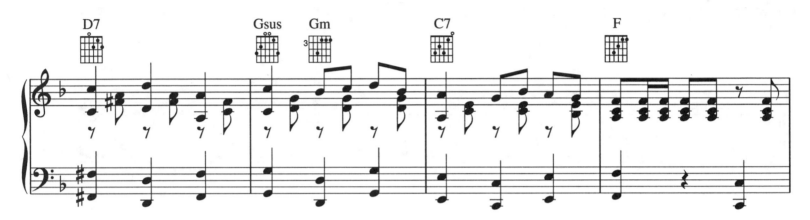

Un dia de San Eu - ge - nio yen - do ha cia el Pra - do le co no -

Wind swirled a - long the high - way when first we met, I re - mem - ber

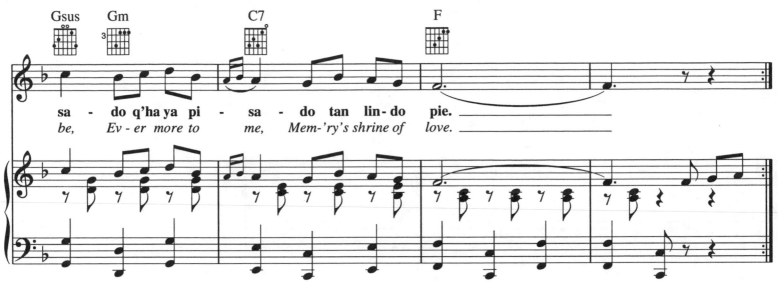

sa - do q'ha ya pi - sa - do tan lin- do pie. _____
be, Ev - er more to me, Mem-'ry's shrine of love. _____

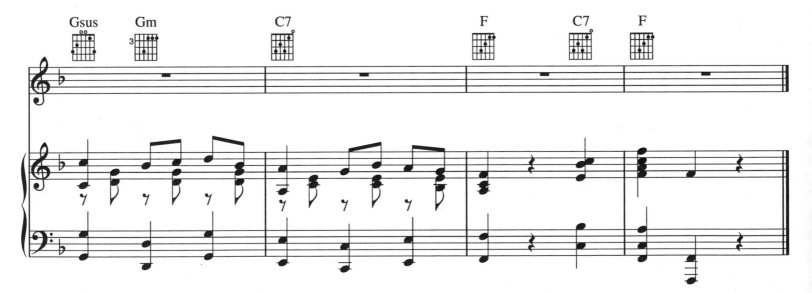

Additional Lyrics

2. Wind blew on the arena when first we met, I remember yet,
Your fight was brave to see, but fear was over me,
Wind was your enemy my Toreador!
Your cape upflying, I saw you lying,
I saw you dying, My Matador.
Then in your dark eyes so deep and tender,
I seemed to recognize, Love's surrender,
and your last greeting, gently enteating,
Set my heart beating, as you said low:
To Chorus

2. Era un Lunes Abrileño el toreaba y a verle fui.
Nunca lo hi cierra que a quella tarde,
De sentimien to crei morir.
Al dar un lance, Cayó en la arena,
Se sintióherido, Miró haciami.
Y un Relicario sacó del pecha,
Que yo enseguidu reconoci,
Cuando el Torero, caia inerte,
En su delirio decia asi:
To Chorus

FEELINGS
(¿Dime?)

English Words and Music by MORRIS ALBERT
Spanish Words by THOMAS FUNDORA

Feel-ings, ___ noth-ing more than feel-ings, ___
¿Di - me? ___ ¿so - la - men - te di - me? ___

try - ing to for - get my feel - ings of
¿Co - mo ol - vi - dar mis sen - ti - mien - tos de_a -

love. Tear-drops ___
mor? Lá - gri - mas ___

never lost you, _____ and feel-ings like I'll
pien-so que ya te he per-di-do, y pre-sien-to que sin

nev - er ____ have you ____ a - gain in my {heart. life.}
tí mi vi-da no ____ no tie-ne ra-zón.

Feel - ings, _____ for all my life I'll
¿Di - me? _____ si siem-pre yo a-

feel it. I wish I've nev-er met you, girl:
sí te a-mé ¿Por-qué a-ho-ra sé lo ton-to que fuí?

FRENESÍ

Words and Music by
ALBERTO DOMINGUEZ

HASTA QUE VUELVAS

Words and Music by MARIO A. RAMOS
and FELIPE BOJAGIL GARZA

len - cio que ol vi - da - ras en mis ma - nos guar - da - ré la es - pe - ra que pin - ta - ron mis po -

e - mas has - ta que vuel - vas _____ a - mor. _____ Has - ta que

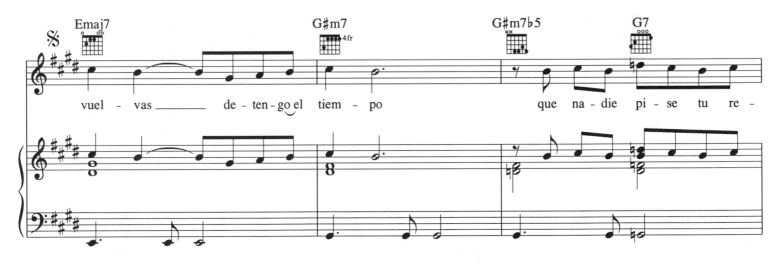

vuel - vas _____ de - ten - go el tiem - po que na - die pi - se tu re -

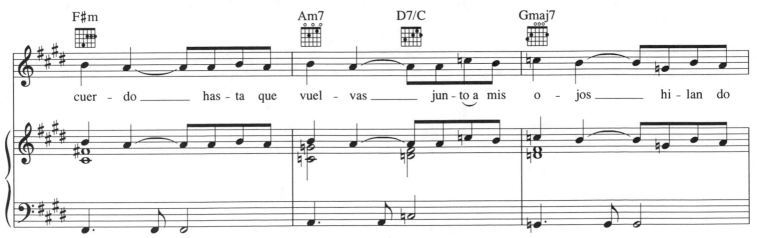

cuer - do _____ has - ta que vuel - vas _____ jun - to a mis o - jos _____ hi - lan do

sue - ños ____ te es - pe - ra - ré. Has - ta que vuel - vas ____ de - ten - go el

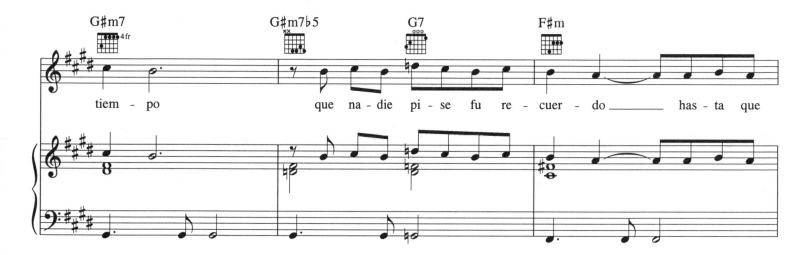

tiem - po ____ que na - die pi - se fu re - cuer - do ____ has - ta que

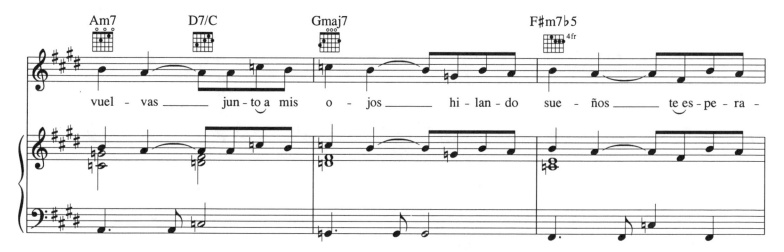

vuel - vas ____ jun - to a mis o - jos ____ hi - lan - do sue - ños ____ te es - pe - ra -

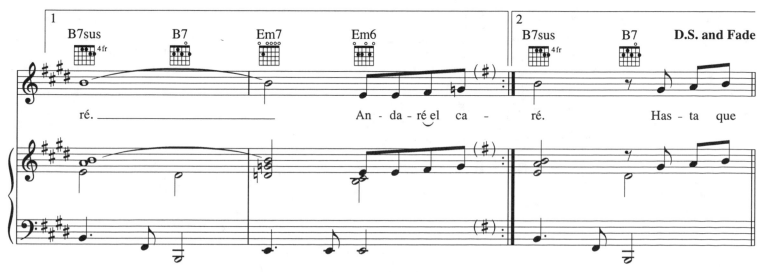

ré. _____ An - da - ré el ca - ré. Has - ta que

HISTORIA DE UN AMOR

Words and Music by
CARLOS ALMARAN

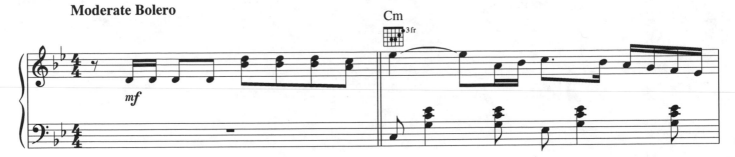

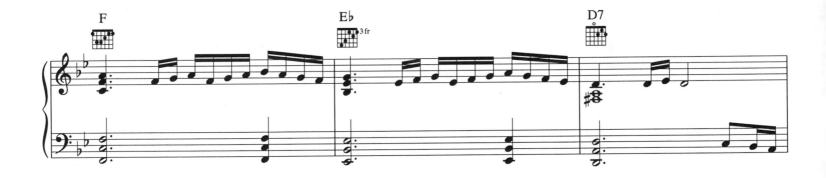

Ya no es-tás más a mi la-do co-ra-zón; _____ en el al-ma so-lo
zón de mi ex-is-tir; _____ a-do-rar-te, pa-ra

ten-go so-le-dad _____ y si yo no pue-do ver-te por qué dios me hi-zo que-
mi fué re-li-gión _____ y en tus be-sos yo en-con-tra-ba el ca-lor que me brin-

rer-te pa-ra ha-cer-me su-frir más. _____ Siem-pre fuis-te la ra-

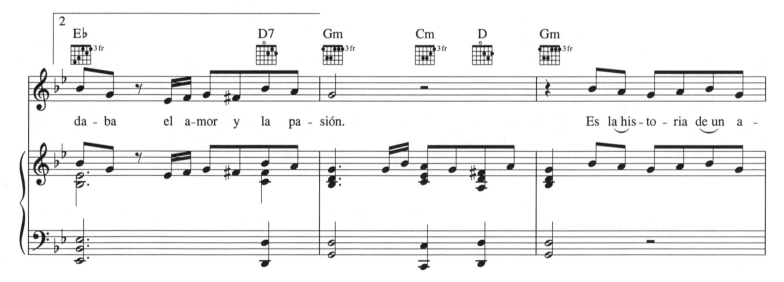

da-ba el a-mor y la pa-sión. Es la his-to-ria de un a-

mor co-mo no hay o-tro i-gual, que me hi-zo com-pren-der to-do el bien to-do el

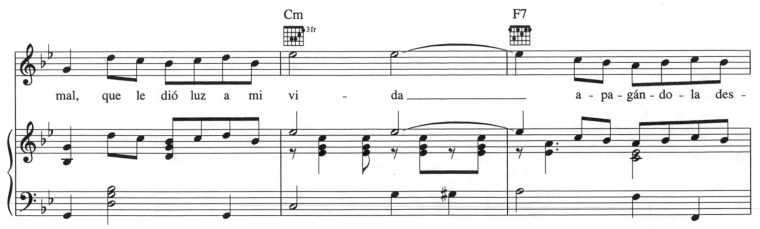

mal, que le dió luz a mi vi - da _____ a - pa - gán - do - la des -

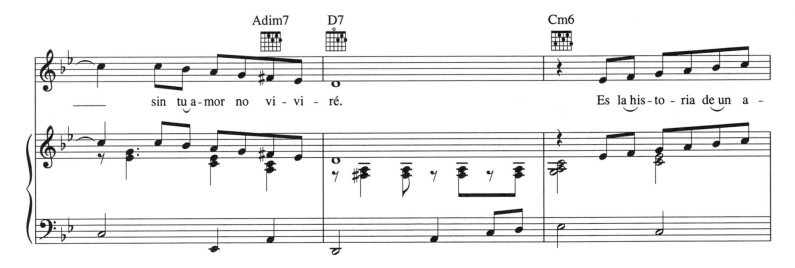

pués. _____ Ay, qué vi - da tan os - cu - ra _____

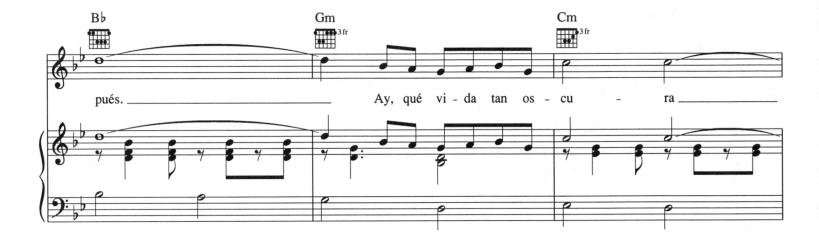

_____ sin tu a - mor no vi - vi - ré. Es la his - to - ria de un a -

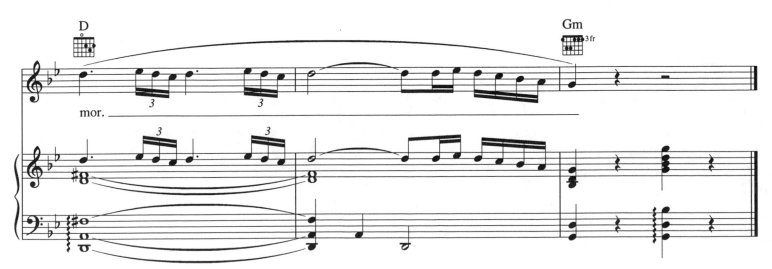

mor. _____

JUVENTUD

by ERNESTO LECUONA

tud, que te vas pa - ra nun - ca vol - ver, ¡que tris - te - za me

dá al ver mi so - le - dad! _____ Ju - ven - tud que te

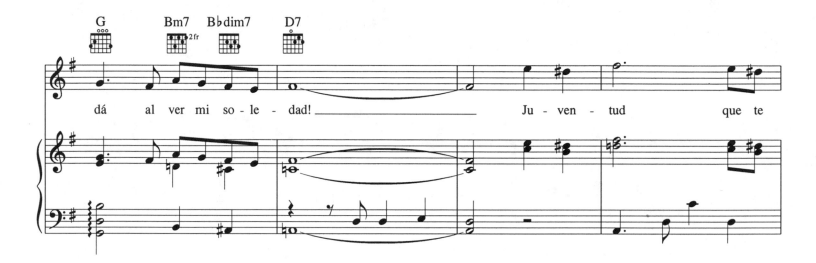

vas y no de - jas en mi ni el re - cuer - do fu - gaz de a - quel in - men - so a -

mor. _____ ¿Pa - ra que re - cor - dar la i - lu - sión de un a -

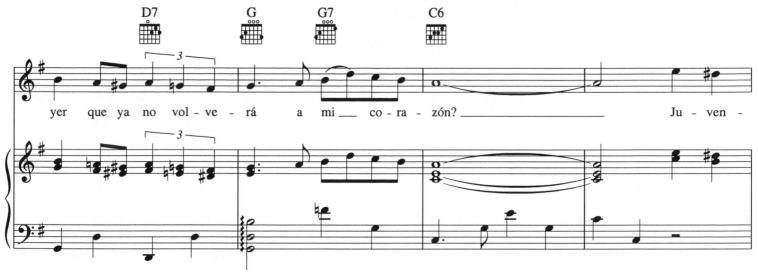

yer que ya no vol-ve-rá a mi __ co-ra-zón? _____ Ju-ven-

tud, te lle-vas-te con-ti-go mi a-mor, el a-

rit. poco a poco

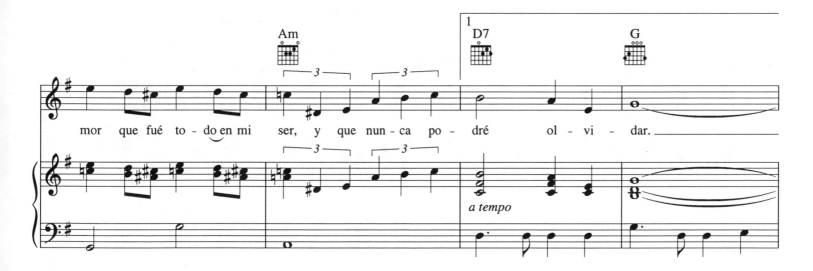

mor que fué to-do en mi ser, y que nun-ca po-dré ol-vi-dar. _____

a tempo

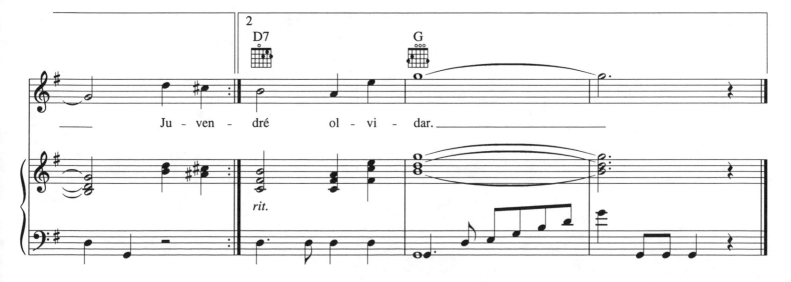

Ju-ven-dré ol-vi-dar. _____

rit.

HOW INSENSITIVE
(Insensatez)

Original Words by VINICIUS DE MORAES
English Words by NORMAN GIMBEL
Music by ANTONIO CARLOS JOBIM

Moderately

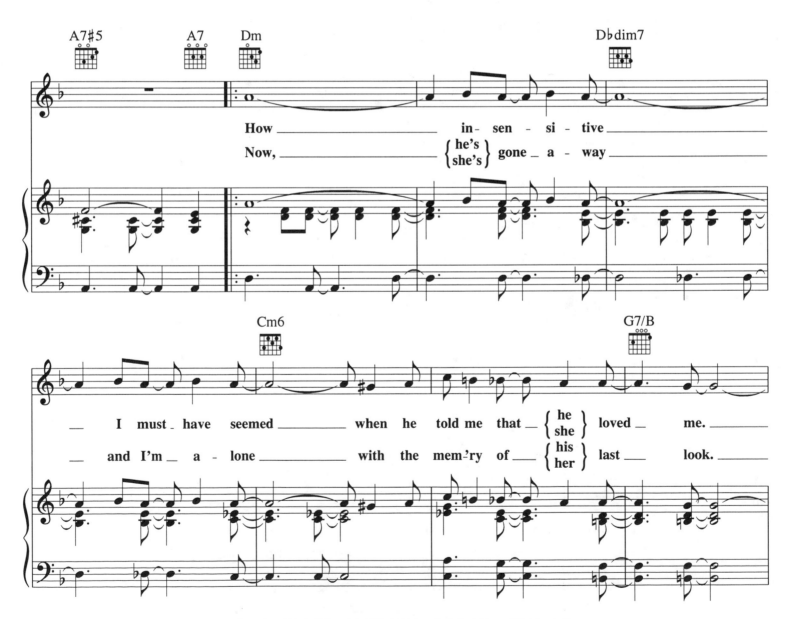

How _____ in-sen-si-tive _____
Now, _____ { he's / she's } gone ___ a ___ way _____

___ I must have seemed _____ when he told me that ___ { he / she } loved ___ me. _____
___ and I'm ___ a - lone _____ with the mem'ry of ___ { his / her } last ___ look. _____

How _____ un - moved __ and cold _____
Vague _____ and drawn __ and sad, _____

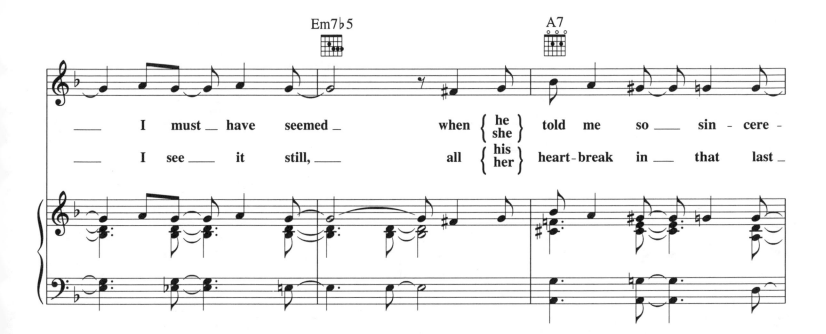

____ I must __ have seemed __ when { he / she } told me so ___ sin - cere -
____ I see __ it still, ___ all { his / her } heart-break in ___ that last __

- ly. _____ Why, _____
__ look. _____ How, _____

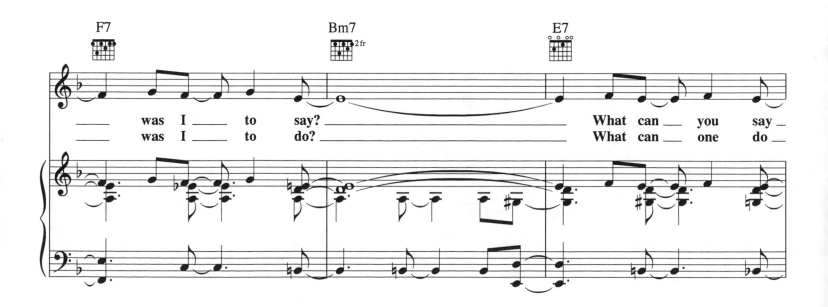

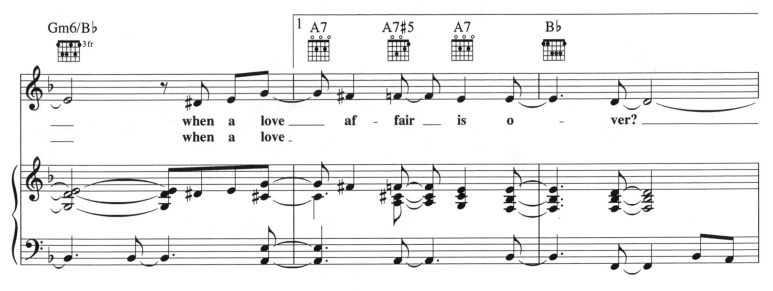

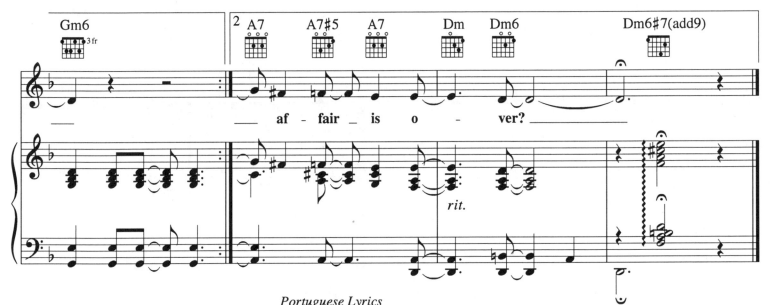

Portuguese Lyrics

A insensatez
Que você fez
Coração mais sem cuidado
Fez chorar de dôr
O seu amôr
Um amôr tão delicado
Ah! Porque você
Foi fraco assim
Assim tão desalmado
Ah! Meu coração
Que nunca amou
Não merece ser amado
Vai meu coração
Ouve a razão
Usa só sinceridade
Quem semeia vento
Diz a razão
Colhe tempestade
Vai meu coração
Pede perdão
Perdão apaixonado
Vai porque
Quem não
Pede perdão
Não é nunca perdoado.

INOLVIDABLE

Words and Music by
JULIO GUTIERREZ

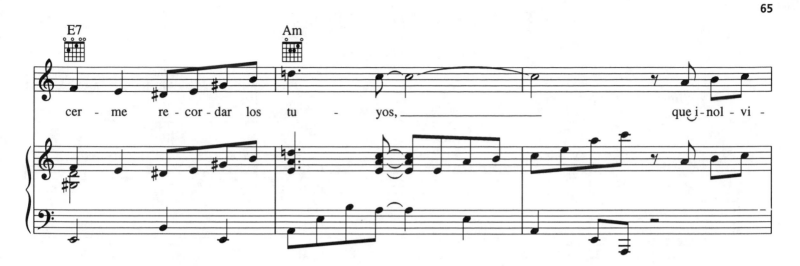

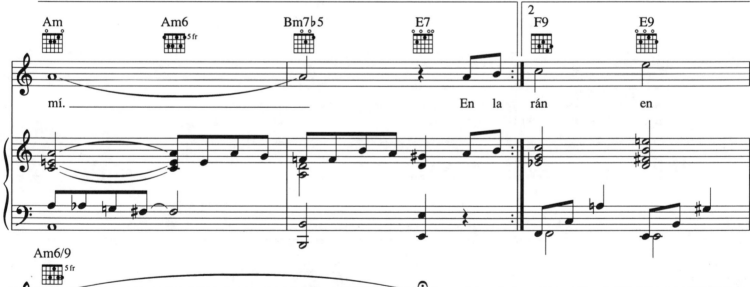

IT'S IMPOSSIBLE
(Somos Novios)

English Lyric by SID WAYNE
Spanish Words and Music by ARMANDO MANZANERO

69

KISS OF FIRE

Words and Music by LESTER ALLEN
and ROBERT HILL
(Adapted from A.G. VILLOLDO)

Moderate Tango

I touch your lips and all at once the sparks go fly-ing. Those dev-il

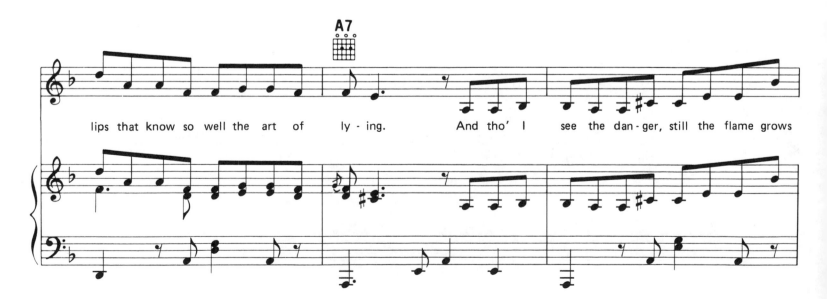

lips that know so well the art of ly-ing. And tho' I see the dan-ger, still the flame grows

MCA Music Publishing

LA COMPARSA
(Carnival Procession)
from DANZAS AFRO-CUBANAS

by ERNESTO LECUONA

Moderate Dance tempo

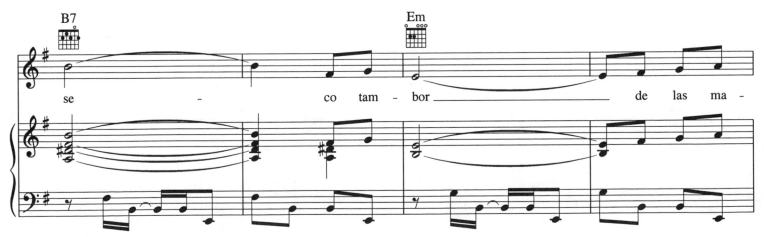

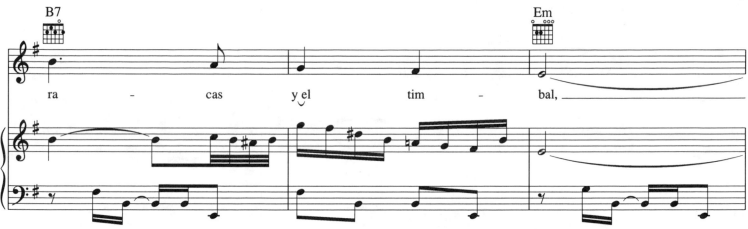

ra - cas y el tim - bal, _____

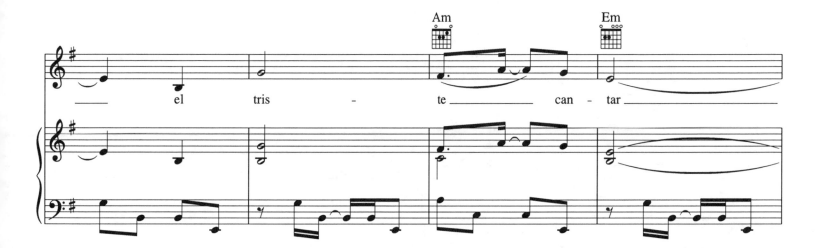

_____ el tris - te _____ can - tar _____

_____ de in - ten - sa e - mo - ción _____

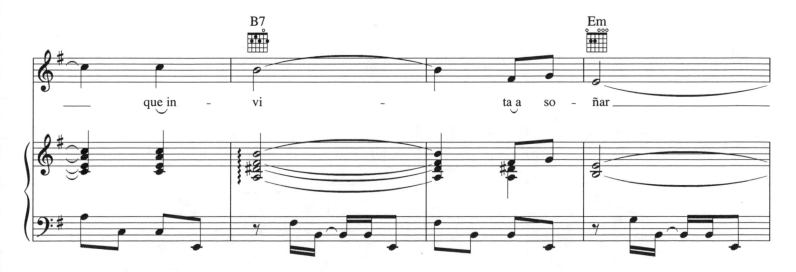

_____ que in - vi - ta a so - ñar _____

al a - mo - ro - so co - ra -

zón. _____ Bri - llan - te y triun -

fal _____ rit - mo ar - mo - nio - so y

sen - sual _____ que in - va - de to - do mi

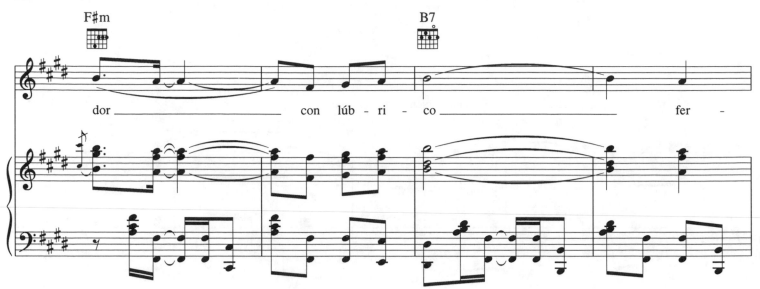

dor _____ con lúb - ri - co _____ fer -

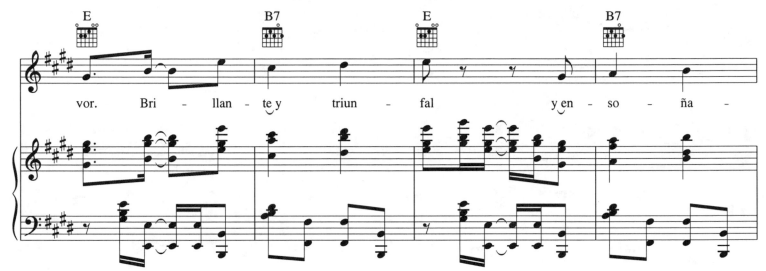

vor. Bri - llan - te y triun - fal y en - so - ña -

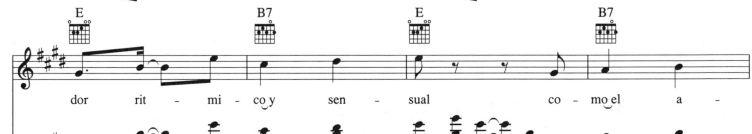

dor rit - mi - co y sen - sual co - mo el a -

mor. _____

rit.

LOVE ME WITH ALL YOUR HEART
(Cuando Calienta El Sol)

English Words by SUNNY SKYLAR
Original Words and Music by CARLOS RIGUAL
and CARLOS A. MARTINOLI

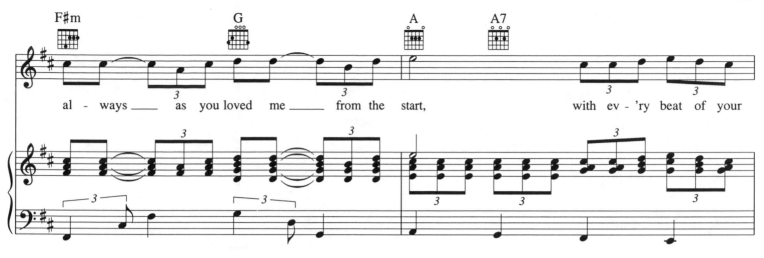

al - ways ___ as you loved me ___ from the start, with ev - 'ry beat of your

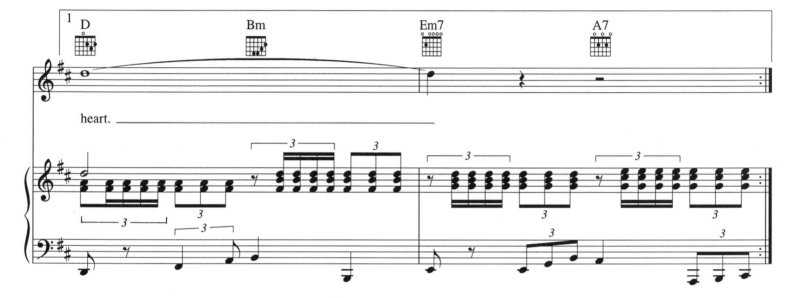

heart. ___

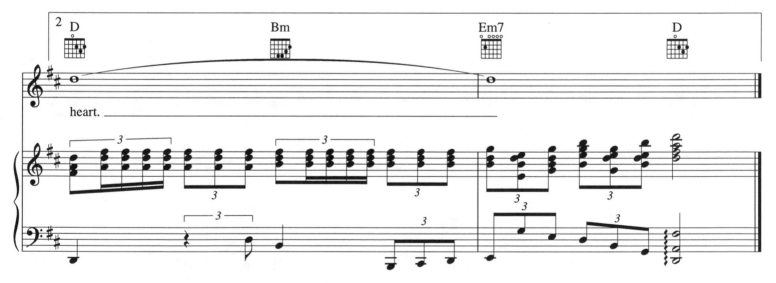

heart. ___

Spanish Lyrics

Cuando calienta el sol aqui en la playa
Siento tu cuerpo vibrar cerca de mí
Es tu palpitar es tu cara es tu pelo
Son tus besos me estremezco - o - o - o
Cuando calienta el sol aqui en la playa
Siento tu cuerpo vibrar cerca de mí
Es tu palpitar tu recuerdo mi locura
Mi delirio me estremezco - o - o - o
Cuando calienta el sol.

MARIA LA O

Music by ERNESTO LECUONA
Lyric by L. WOLFE GILBERT

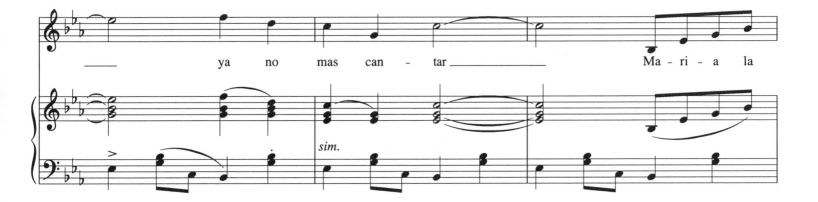

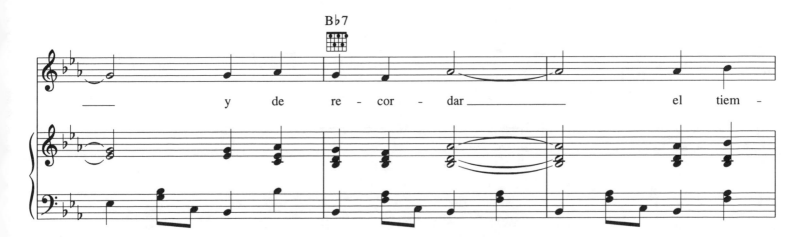

po fe - liz _____ de tus be - sos que fu -

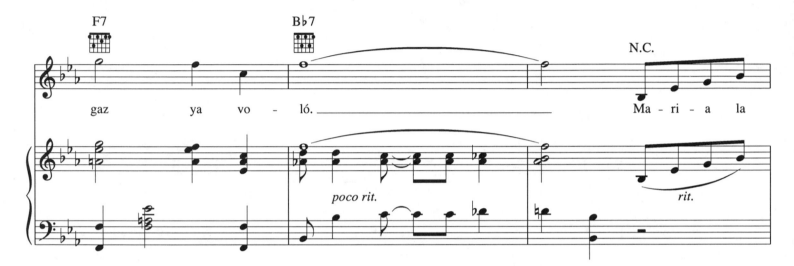

gaz ya vo - ló. _____ Ma - ri - a la

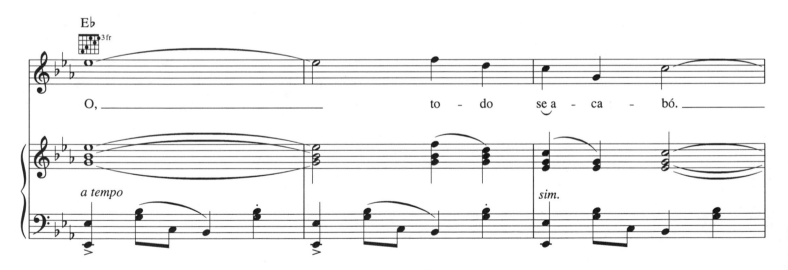

O, _____ to - do se a - ca - bó. _____

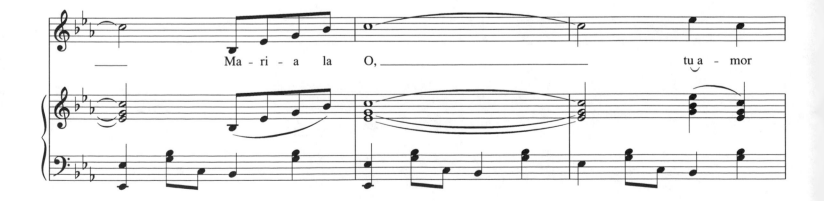

Ma - ri - a la O, _____ tu a - mor

MEDITATION
(Meditacáo)

Original Words by NEWTON MENDONCA
Music by ANTONIO CARLOS JOBIM
English Words by NORMAN GIMBEL

MCA Music Publishing

MORE
(Ti Guardero' Nel Cuore)
from the film MONDO CANE

Music by NINO OLIVIERO and RIZ ORTOLANI
Italian Lyrics by MARCELLO CIORCIOLINI
English Lyrics by NORMAN NEWELL

Lyrics:

More than the great-est love the world has known;
this is the love I'll give to you a-lone.
More than the sim-ple words I try to say;

Se tu mi guar-di in fon-do al cuor, ve-
drai Un no-me scrit-to con le nu-vo-le
Che om-bre di-se-gna-no di fa-vo-la

MUCHO CORAZÓN

Words and Music by
EMMA ELENA VALDELAMAR

Moderate Bolero

Dí si en-con-tras-te _____ en mi pa-sa-do _____ u-na ra-

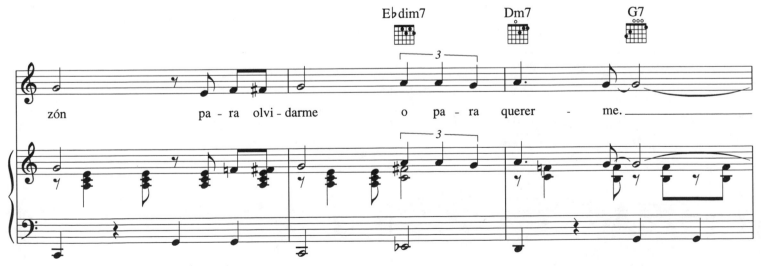

zón _____ pa-ra olvi-darme o pa-ra querer-me. _____

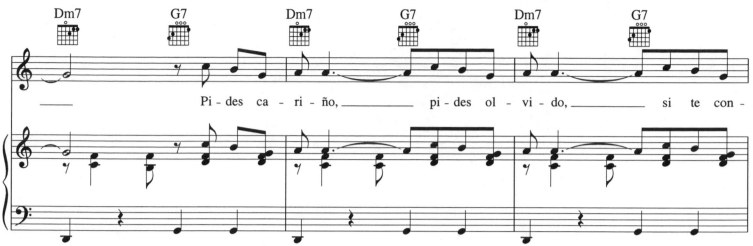

Pi - des ca - ri - ño, _____ pi - des ol - vi - do, _____ si te con -

vie - ne _____ no lla - mes co - ra - zón _____

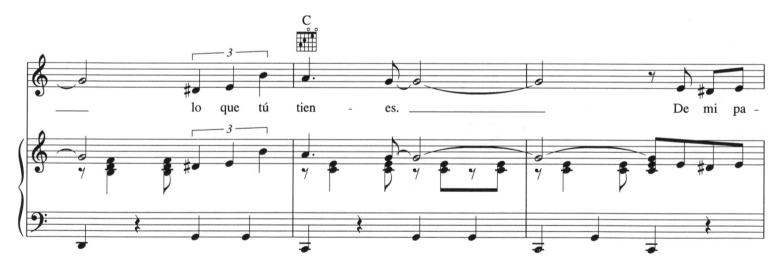

lo que tú tien - es. _____ De mi pa -

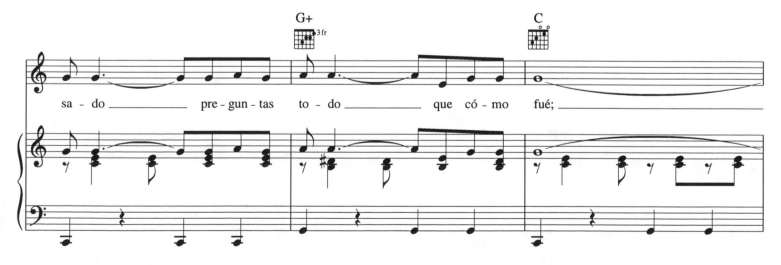

sa - do _____ pre - gun - tas to - do _____ que có - mo fué;

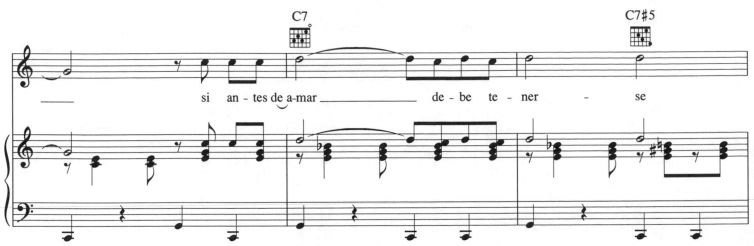

si an - tes de a-mar _____ de - be te - ner __ se

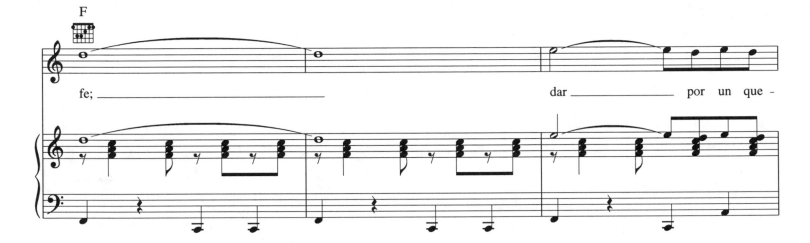

fe; _____ dar _____ por un que -

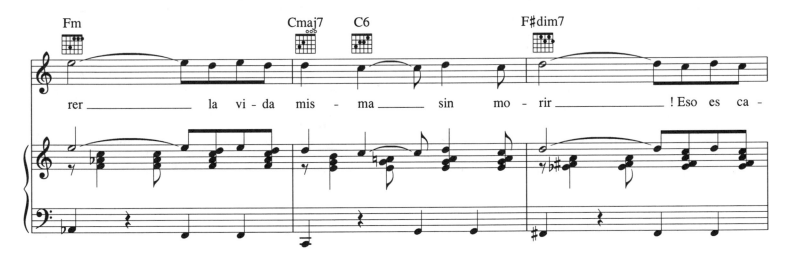

rer _____ la vi - da mis - ma _____ sin mo - rir _____ ! Eso es ca -

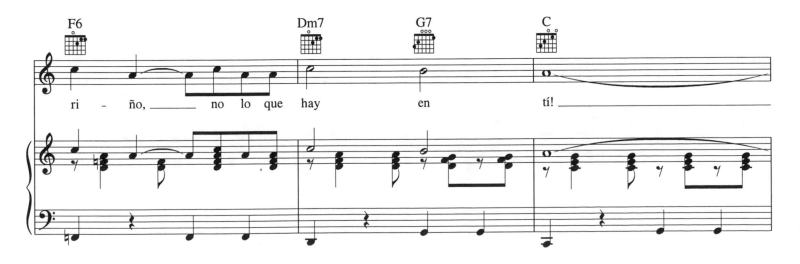

ri - ño, _____ no lo que hay en tí! _____

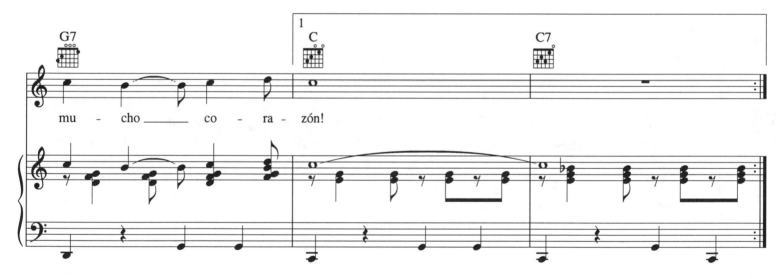

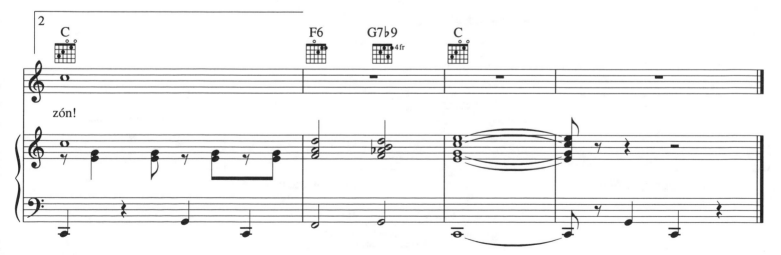

NOCHE AZUL
(Blue Night)

by ERNESTO LECUONA

No - che a - zul, que en _ mi al - ma re - fle - jó la pa - sión que _ so - ña - ba a - ca - ri - ciar,

vuel - ve de nue - vo a ___ dar

Bb6

F6

paz a mi ___ co - ra - zón. ¿No ves que

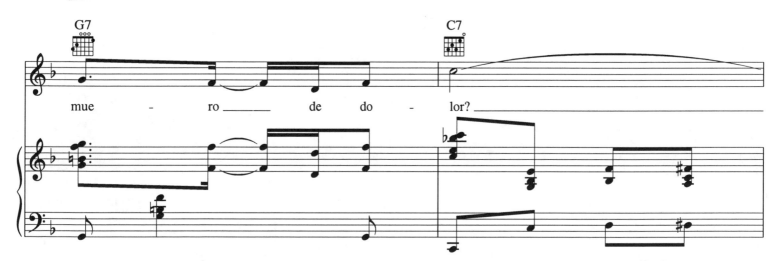

G7

C7

mue - ro ___ de do - lor? ___

1

2

F6

___ Ven ___ no-che a - zul, ___ ven o - tra

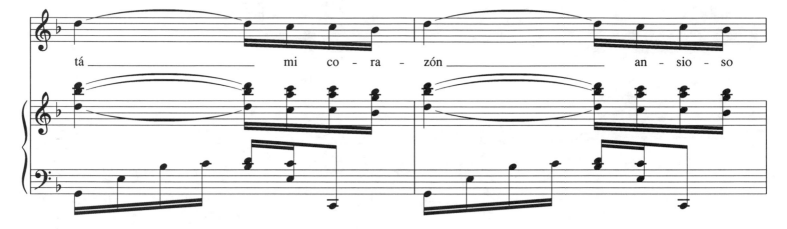

NOCHE DE RONDA
(Be Mine Tonight)

Words and Music by
MARIA TERESA LARA

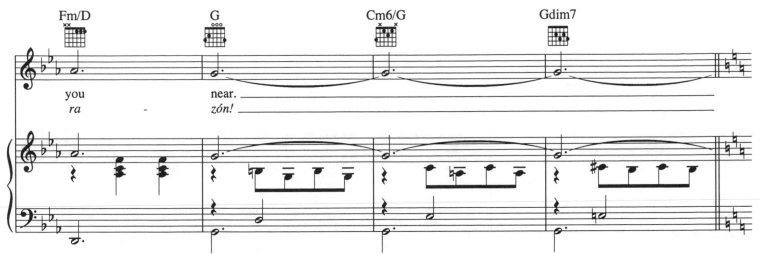

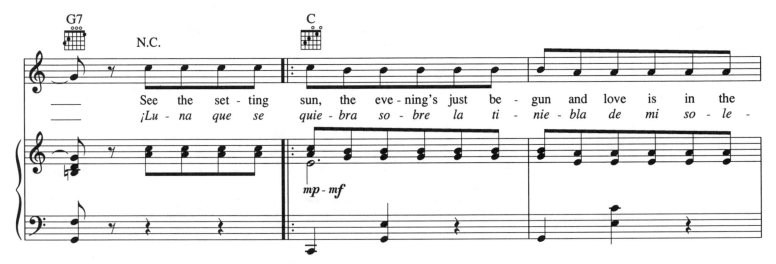

Whis-per love words, _____ oh, so ten - der, _____
que las ron - das _____ no son bue - nas,

Give your kiss - es _____ in sur - ren - der,
que ha - cen da - ño, _____ que dan pe - nas,

Let your heart be mine to -
que se a - ca - ba mi por llo -

night. _____
rar. _____

See the set - ting night. _____
¡Lu - na que se rar.

POR ESO TE QUIERO

English Lyric by ALBERT STILLMAN
Spanish Words and Music by ERNESTO LECUONA

quie - ro _____ por que se que llo - ras - te _____

_____ en mis di - as de au - sen - cia _____ de tris - te so - le -

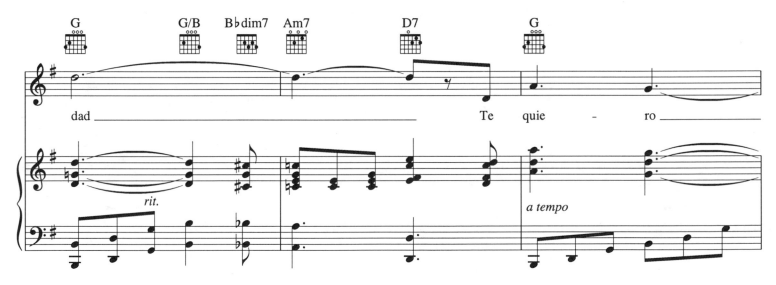

dad _____ Te quie - ro _____

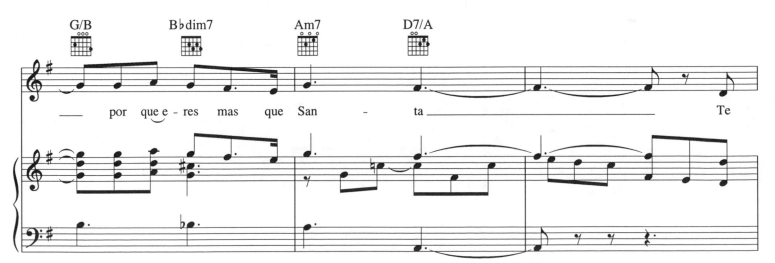

_____ por que e - res mas que San - ta _____ Te

quie - ro _____ por que e - res mi a - le - gri - a _____

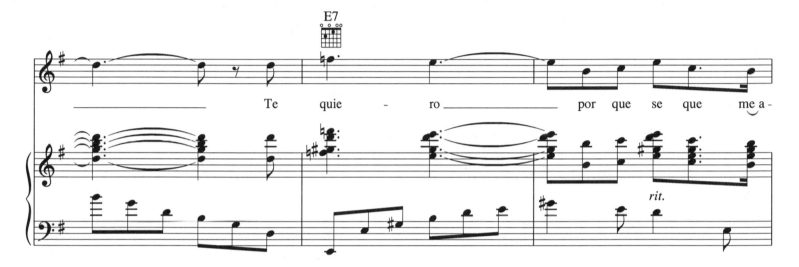

_____ Te quie - ro _____ por que se que me a -

do - ras _____ Te quie - ro _____

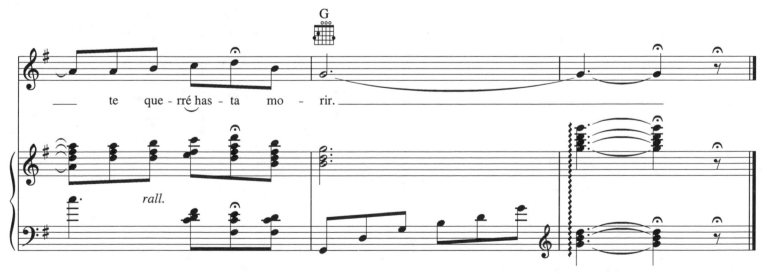

_____ te que - rré has - ta mo - rir. _____

OUR LANGUAGE OF LOVE
from IRMA LA DOUCE

Music by MARGUERITE MONNOT
Original French words by ALEXANDRE BREFFORT
English words by JULIAN MORE, DAVID HENEKER and MONTY NORMAN

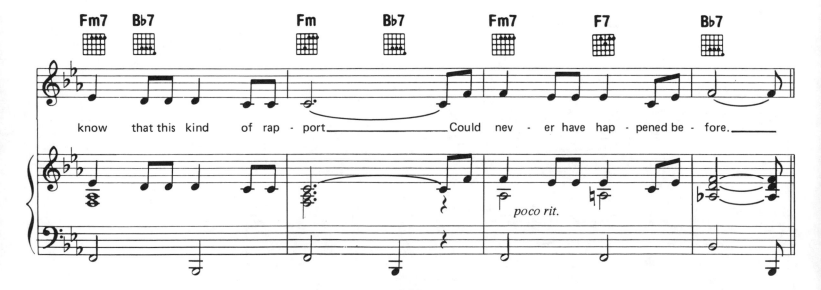

QUIET NIGHTS OF QUIET STARS
(Corcovado)

English Words by GENE LEES
Original Words and Music by
ANTONIO CARLOS JOBIM

Moderately slow

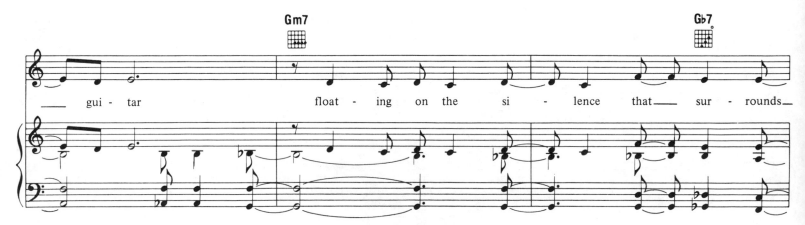

MCA Music Publishing

SWAY
(Quien Será)

English Words by NORMAN GIMBEL
Spanish Words and Music by
PABLO BELTRAN RUIZ

SPANISH EYES

Words by CHARLES SINGLETON and EDDIE SNYDER
Music by BERT KAEMPFERT

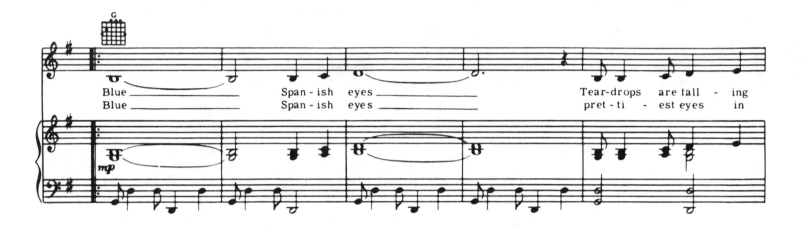

Blue _____ Span - ish eyes _____ Tear-drops are fall - ing
Blue _____ Span - ish eyes _____ pret - ti - est eyes in

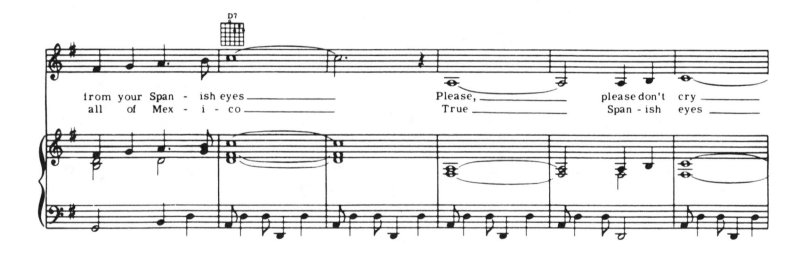

from your Span - ish eyes _____ Please, _____ please don't cry _____
all of Mex - i - co _____ True _____ Span - ish eyes _____

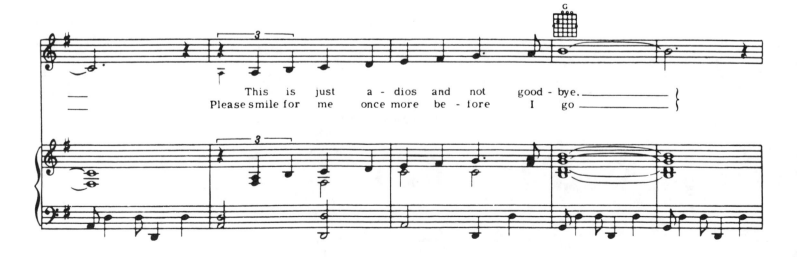

This is just a - dios and not good - bye. _____
Please smile for me once more be - fore I go _____

Soon _____ I'll re - turn _____ Bring-ing you all the

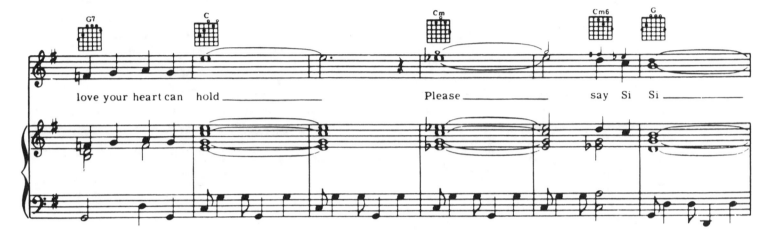

love your heart can hold _____ Please _____ say Si Si _____

Say you and your Span-ish eyes will wait for me. _____ Span-ish eyes _____

Wait for me, say Si Si! _____

TANGO OF ROSES

Words by MARJORIE HARPER
Music by VITTORIO MASCHERONI

Chorus

pas-sion, ro-mance, and love._____ Ros - es try_____

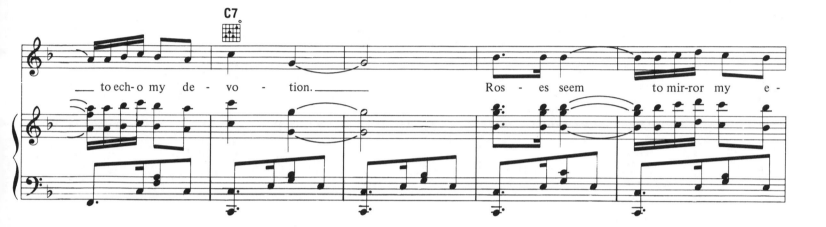

_____ to ech-o my de - vo - tion._____ Ros - es seem to mir-ror my e -

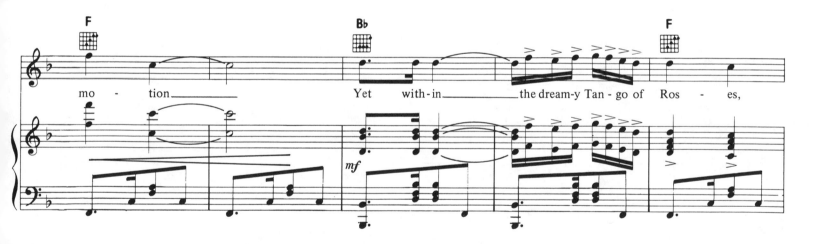

mo - tion_____ Yet with-in_____ the dream-y Tan - go of Ros - es,

My heart so will-ing-ly dis - clos - es; Love will out-live the rose.

TRES PALABRAS
(Without You)

Original Words and Music by OSVALDO FARRES
English Words by RAY GILBERT

Moderately

I'm so lone-ly and blue, _____ when I'm with-
O - ye la con-fe - sión, _____ de mi se -

out you. _____ I don't know what I'd do, _____
cre - to, _____ na - ce de un co - ra - zón

_____ sweet-heart, with - out you. _____ The joy and
_____ qe es - ta de - sier - to; _____ Con tres pa -

TU FELICIDAD
(Made for Each Other)

Original Words and Music by
RENE TOUZET
English Words by ERVIN DRAKE and JIMMY SHIRL

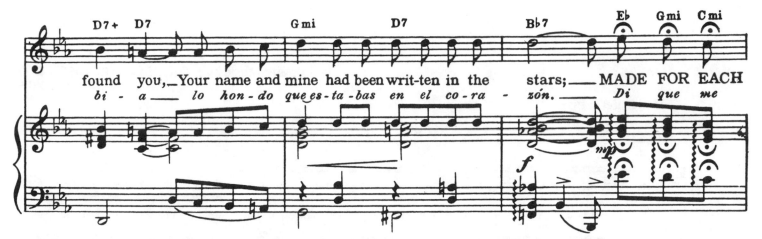

found you,__Your name and mine had been writ-ten in the stars;__ MADE FOR EACH
bi - a__ lo hon-do que es-ta-bas en el co-ra - zón.__ Di que me

OTH - ER__ like sun and sky,__ We'll have each oth - er__ as years go
quie - res __ a - sí, a - sí __ di co-mo en - ton - ces __ que e res fe -

by,__ We'll share to - geth - er the dreams that you and I MADE FOR EACH
liz __ por-que mi vi - da no es vi - da si no es TU FE - LI -

OTH - ER! MADE FOR EACH OTH - ER!__
CI - DAD Di que me CI - DAD.__

UNO

Words and Music by ENRIQUE SANTOS DISCEPOLO
and MARIANO MORES

Moderate Tango

U - no, bus - ca lle - no de es - pe - ran - zas, el ca - mi - no que los sue - ños pro - me - tie - ron a sus

an - sias... Sa - be que la lu - cha es cruel y es mu - cha, pe - ro lu - cha y se de -

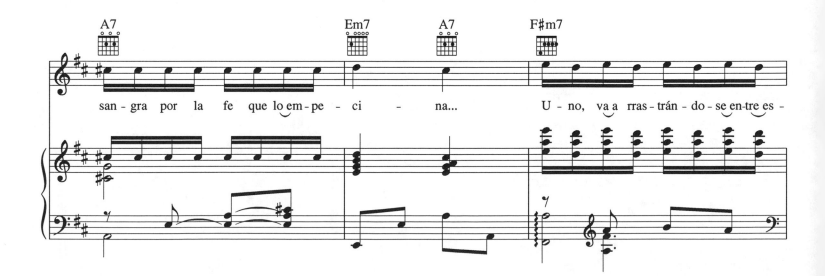

san - gra por la fe que lo em - pe - ci - na... U - no, va a rras - trán - do - se en - tre es -

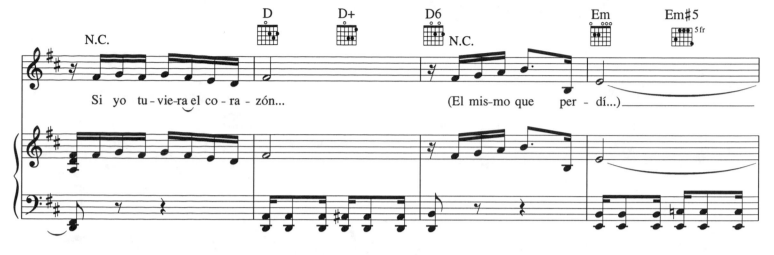

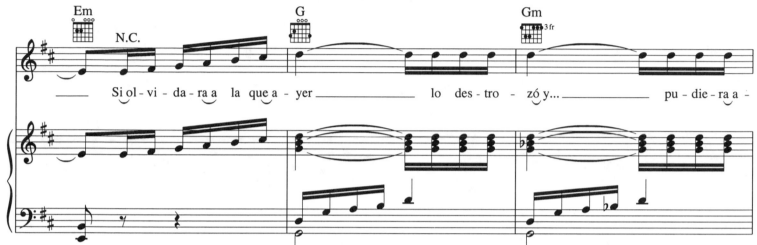

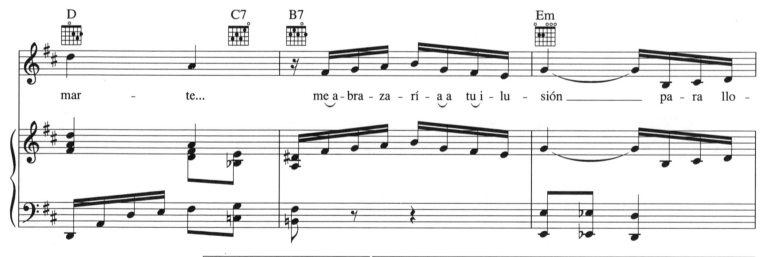

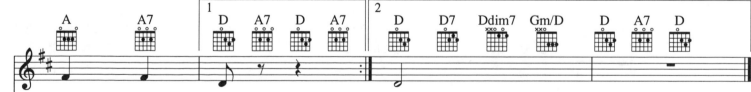

VOY A APAGAR LA LUZ

Words and Music by
ARMANDO MANZANERO

pue - de, don - de no hay im - po - si - bles, ___ qué im -

por - ta vi - vir de i - lu - sió - nes si a - sí soy fe - liz.

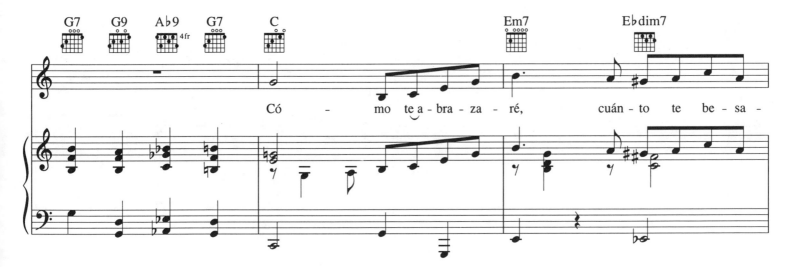

Có - mo te a - bra - za - ré, cuán - to te be - sa -

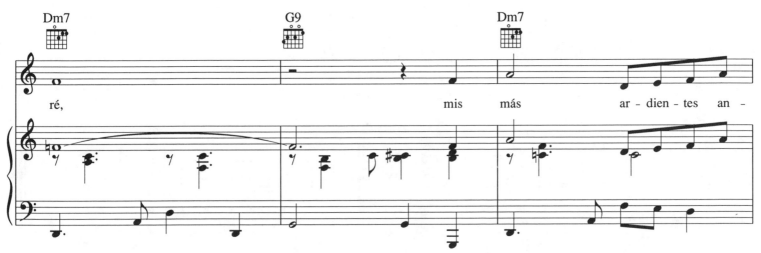

ré, mis más ar - dien - tes an -

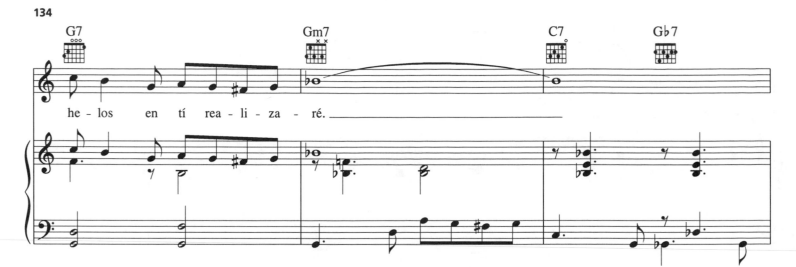

he - los en tí rea - li - za - ré. _____

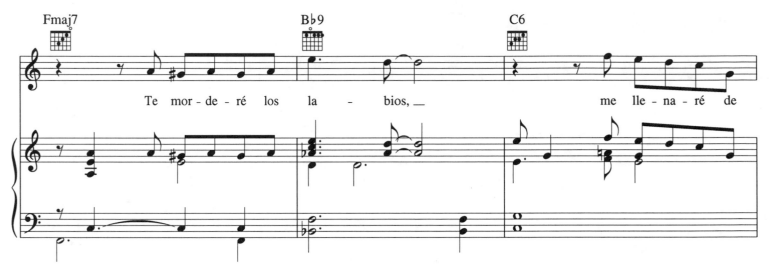

Te mor-de - ré los la - bios, ___ me lle - na - ré de

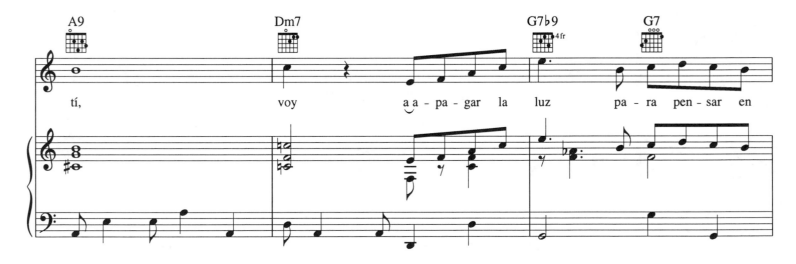

tí, voy a a - pa - gar la luz pa - ra pen - sar en

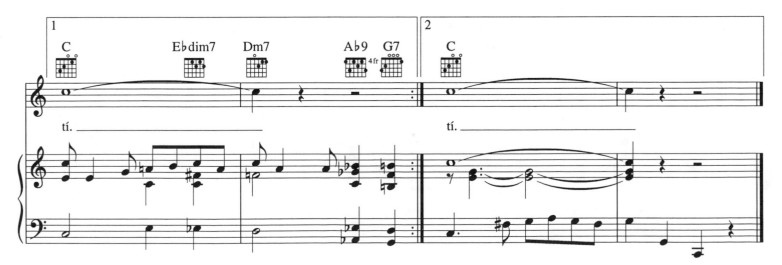

tí. _____   tí. _____

WHAT A DIFF'RENCE A DAY MADE

English Words by STANLEY ADAMS
Music and Spanish Words by MARIA GREVER

YOU BELONG TO MY HEART

(Solamente Una Vez)

Music and Spanish Words by AGUSTIN LARA
English Words by RAY GILBERT

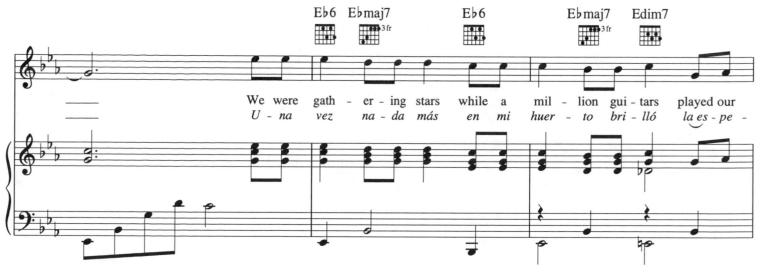

We were gath-er-ing stars while a mil-lion gui-tars played our
U - na vez na - da más en mi huer - to bri - lló la es - pe -

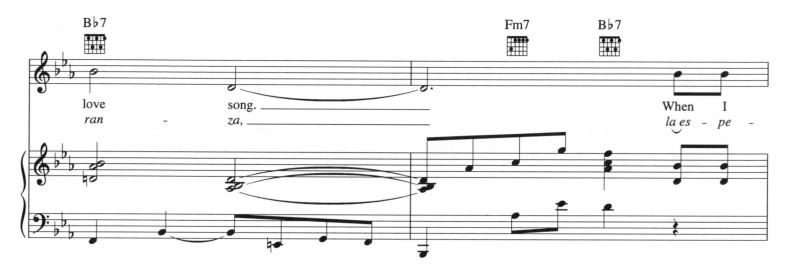

love song. _____
ran - za, _____

When I
la es - pe -

said, "I love you," ev-'ry beat of my heart said it
ran - za que a - lum - bra el ca - mi - no de mi so - le -
too. _____
dad. _____

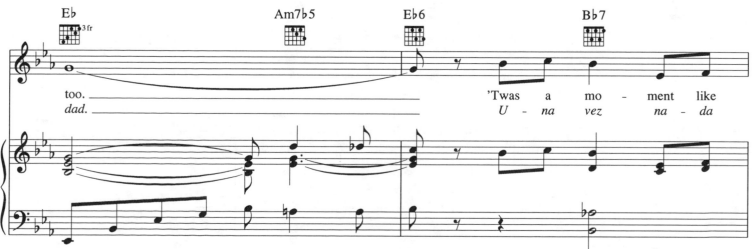

'Twas a mo - ment like
U - na vez na - da

YOURS
(Cuando Se Quiere De Veras)

Words by ALBERT GAMSE and JACK SHERR
Music by GONZALO ROIG

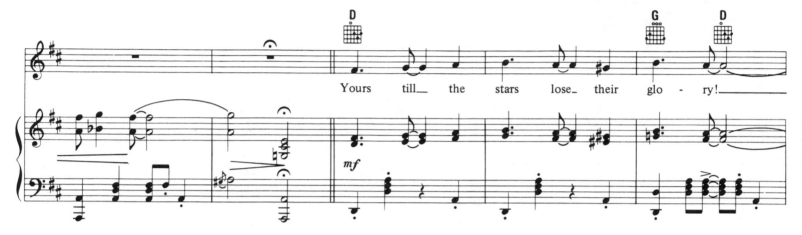

Yours till the stars lose their glo - ry!

Yours till the birds fail to sing!

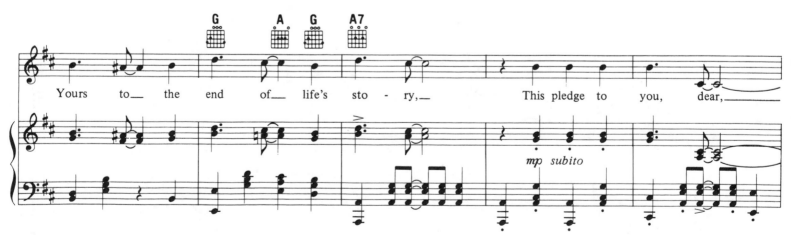

Yours to the end of life's sto - ry, This pledge to you, dear,

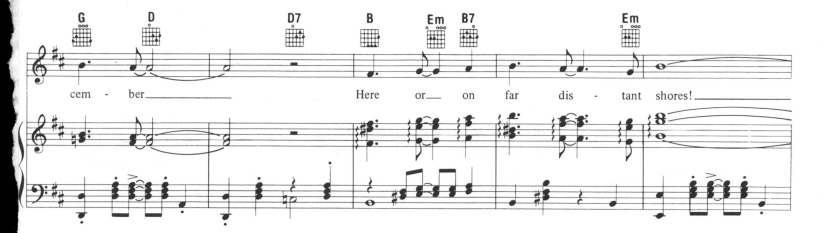

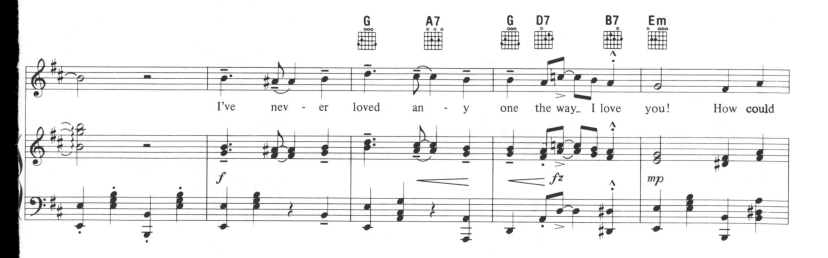

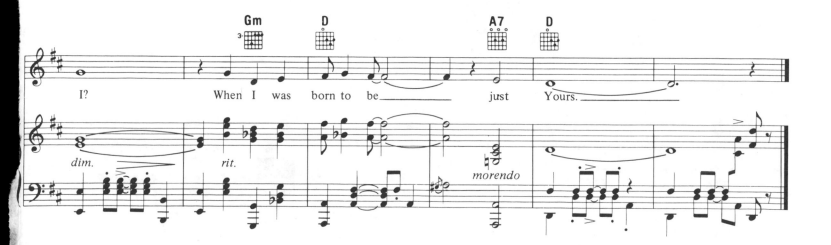

BIG BOOKS OF MUSIC

Our "Big Books" feature big selections of popular titles under one cover, perfect for performing musicians, holiday sing-alongs, and music aficionados. All books are arranged for piano, voice, and guitar, and feature stay-open binding, so the books lie flat without breaking the spine.

BIG BOOK OF CHILDREN'S SONGS

61 songs that children know and love! The P/V/G edition features a categorical listing of songs and ideas for musical and educational activities. Includes: The Alphabet Song • Happy Birthday To You • I Whistle A Happy Tune • It's A Small World • London Bridge • Mickey Mouse March • Old MacDonald Had A Farm • Peter Cottontail • The Rainbow Connection • Supercalifragilisticexpialidocious • This Land Is Your Land • and more!
00359261.................................$12.95

GREAT BIG BOOK OF CHILDREN'S SONGS

74 classics for kids, including: ABC-DEF-GHI • Beauty And The Beast • Bein' Green • The Brady Bunch • "C" Is For Cookie • The Candy Man • Casper The Friendly Ghost • Everything Is Beautiful • I'm Popeye The Sailor Man • Kum Ba Yah • Let's Go Fly A Kite • The Marvelous Toy • Puff The Magic Dragon • Rubber Duckie • A Spoonful Of Sugar • Take Me Out To The Ballgame • Under The Sea • Won't You Be My Neighbor? • and more.
00310002.................................$14.95

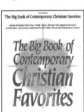

BIG BOOK OF CONTEMPORARY CHRISTIAN FAVORITES

A comprehensive collection of 50 songs, including: Angels • El Shaddai • Friends • The Great Adventure • I Will Be Here • Love In Any Language • Love Will Be Our Home • O Magnify The Lord • People Need The Lord • Say The Name • Turn Up The Radio • Via Dolorosa • Whatever You Ask • Where There Is Faith • and more.
00310021.................................$19.95

BIG BOOK OF COUNTRY MUSIC

Includes over 60 classic and contemporary country hits: Ain't Going Down ('Til the Sun Comes Up) • Before You Kill Us All • Blue • The Greatest Man I Never Knew • I Can Love You Like That • I've Come to Expect It From You • The Keeper of the Stars • No One Else on Earth • On the Other Hand • One Boy, One Girl • Ring on Her Finger, Time on Her Hands • She's Not the Cheatin' Kind • When You Say Nothing at All • Wild Angels • more.
00310188.................................$19.95

THE BIG BOOK OF BROADWAY

Songs from over 50 shows, including *Annie Get Your Gun, Carousel, Company, Guys And Dolls, Les Miserables, South Pacific, Sunset Boulevard,* and more. 76 classics, including: All I Ask Of You • Bali Ha'i • Bring Him Home • Camelot • Don't Cry For Me Argentina • Hello, Young Lovers • I Dreamed A Dream • The Impossible Dream • Mame • Memory • Oklahoma • One • People • Tomorrow • Unusual Way • and more.
00311658.................................$19.95

BIG BOOK OF LATIN AMERICAN SONGS

90 favorites in their original languages, including: Amapola • Andalucia • The Breeze And I • Cherry Pink & Apple Blossom White • Desafinado • Don't Cry For Me Argentina • Flamingo • The Girl From Ipanema • How Insensitive • Kiss Of Fire • La Cucaracha • La Paloma • Little Boat • Malaguena • Meditation • Miami Beach Rumba • One Note Samba • Poinciana • Que Sera Sera • Quiet Nights Of Quiet Stars • Samba De Orfeu • So Nice (Summer Samba) • South Of The Border • Tango Of Roses • Yellow Days • Vaya Con Dios • and more!
00311562.................................$19.95

THE BIG BOOK OF NOSTALGIA

More than 160 of the best songs ever written, complete with a brief history of each song, including: After The Ball • After You've Gone • Anchors Aweigh • Ballin' The Jack • Beale Street Blues • The Bells Of St. Mary's • The Entertainer • Fascination • Give My Regards To Broadway • I Ain't Got Nobody • I Wonder Who's Kissing Her Now • Let Me Call You Sweetheart • Meet Me In St. Louis, Louis • My Wild Irish Rose • Sidewalks Of New York • When Irish Eyes Are Smiling • You Made Me Love You • and more.
00310004.................................$19.95

THE BIG BOOK OF STANDARDS

86 classics essential to any music library, including: April In Paris • Autumn In New York • Blue Skies • Cheek To Cheek • Heart And Soul • I Left My Heart In San Francisco • In The Mood • Isn't It Romantic? • It's Impossible • L-O-V-E • Lover, Come Back To Me • Mona Lisa • Moon River • The Nearness Of You • Out Of Nowhere • Spanish Eyes • Star Dust • Stella By Starlight • That Old Black Magic • They Say It's Wonderful • The Way We Were • What Now My Love • and more.
00311667.................................$19.95

BIG BOOK OF CHRISTMAS SONGS

An outstanding collection of over 125 all-time Christmas classics, including: Angels We Have Heard On High • Auld Lang Syne • The Boar's Head Carol • Coventry Carol • Deck The Hall • The First Noel • The Friendly Beasts • God Rest Ye Merry Gentlemen • I Heard The Bells On Christmas Day • Jesu, Joy Of Man's Desiring • Joy To The World • Masters In This Hall • O Holy Night • The Story Of The Shepherd • 'Twas The Night Before Christmas • What Child Is This? • and many more.
00311520.................................$19.95

BIG BOOK OF LOVE AND WEDDING SONGS

Over 80 wedding favorites, including: All I Ask Of You • Anniversary Song • Ave Maria • Could I Have This Dance • Dedicated To The One I Love • Endless Love • Forever And Ever, Amen • Here And Now • Longer • Lost In Your Eyes • So In Love • Something • Sunrise, Sunset • Through The Years • Trumpet Voluntary • The Vows Go Unbroken • You Decorated My Life • and more.
00311567.................................$19.95

THE BIG BOOK OF JAZZ

75 of the world's greatest jazz classics, including: Autumn Leaves • Bewitched • Birdland • Cherokee • A Fine Romance • Flying Home • Have You Met Miss Jones • Honeysuckle Rose • How High The Moon • (I Can Recall) Spain • I've Got You Under My Skin • Jelly Roll Blues • Lullaby Of Birdland • Morning Dance • A Night In Tunisia • A Nightingale Sang In Berkeley Square • Route 66 • Take The "A" Train • and more.
00311557.................................$19.95

BIG BOOK OF MOVIE AND TV THEMES

Over 90 familiar themes, including: Alfred Hitchcock Theme • Beauty And The Beast • Candle On The Water • Theme From E.T. • Endless Love • Hawaii Five-O • I Love Lucy • Theme From Jaws • Jetsons • Major Dad Theme • The Masterpiece • Mickey Mouse March • The Munsters Theme • Theme From Murder, She Wrote • Mystery • Somewhere Out There • Unchained Melody • Won't You Be My Neighbor • and more!
00311582.................................$19.95

THE BIG BOOK OF ROCK

78 of rock's biggest hits, including: Addicted To Love • American Pie • Born To Be Wild • Cold As Ice • Dust In The Wind • Free Bird • Goodbye Yellow Brick Road • Groovin' • Hey Jude • I Love Rock N Roll • Lay Down Sally • Layla • Livin' On A Prayer • Louie Louie • Maggie May • Me And Bobby McGee • Monday, Monday • Owner Of A Lonely Heart • Shout • Walk This Way • We Didn't Start The Fire • You Really Got Me • and more.
00311566.................................$19.95

Prices, contents, and availability subject to change without notice.

FOR MORE INFORMATION, SEE YOUR LOCAL MUSIC DEALER, OR WRITE TO:

HAL•LEONARD® CORPORATION
7777 W. BLUEMOUND RD. P.O. BOX 13819 MILWAUKEE, WI 53213